My Spiritual Revelations and other BS

Brother Bob

Permette Publishing
(permettepublishing@verizon.net)

My Spiritual Revelations and other BS

Published by Permette Publishing

Copyright © 2006

First edition

ISBN 978-0-6151-3750-6

Thank you Courtney, Lalo, Jeanne, Becky, Tina, Andrew, David and Rod

Preface

"You should write a book," many non-writers have heard friends extol in response to their tall tales. I heard it many times during the nearly 27 years that I ran my health food restaurant, *Food For Thought*. Usually, these comments were in response to my telling some dramatic tale of past events to a new crop of workers. The stories were easy to tell, but to write a book was far too daunting a task for me. Maybe someday I would dictate one to a ghost writer, but to actually write something myself was out of the question.

A couple of months ago, a coworker of my wife gave her a lovely present – a handmade notebook with blank pages that she had constructed herself. As my wife showed me the beautifully bound book, she commented that she couldn't possibly use it as a common notebook. At that moment something went off in my brain. "Give it to me. I'll write a book." This is that book.

2004

CONTENTS

Part One - Learning
    Number One - Humor   5
    Number Two - The Unbeliever   7
    Number Three - Faith   9
Part Two - Opinion
    Number One - The Bible   13
    Number Two - God   15
    Number Three - Jesus   17
Part Three - Experiences
    Number One - The First Time   21
    Number Two - Altered Mind   25
    Number Three - The Air Conditioner   27
    Number Four - The Accident   33
    Number Five - The Dream   37
    Number Six - The Game   39
Part Four - Other BS   41
Part Five - Love Poems   45
Part Six - More BS   55

My Spiritual Revelations

and other BS

Brother Bob

Part One

Learning

Number One

Humor

Over 45 years ago when I was in the minor seminary, I was told that there were several traits that were important to becoming a priest. One of them was a total surprise to me: a sense of humor. I had always thought that all traditional religions approach spirituality with piety, not humor. But humor seemed a much better way to fly.

When the Christ supposedly cried out shortly before he died and someone thought he might need something for the pain, like a vinegar soaked sponge, it was not written down for posterity as something analogous to "He could sure use some Tylenol with codeine." Why not? Would that have given it less meaning?

Over 30 years ago, my son would ask me to read the Bible. Why? Because he was spiritually motivated? No, because the way I read it was a riot. I can't even remember how I did it but no matter what passage I read, we were in stitches. Whatever points the writer was trying to make had almost no relevance. The words became absurdities and were hilarious. He would giggle and giggle and plead, "Read more. Read more."

It now appears to me that the humor that erupted, brought wisdom straight to the soul and bypassed the mind.

Number Two

The Unbeliever

When I was a young man, I had a casual friend who was a non-believer. I admired him. I had been raised a Catholic with lots of rules, virtues, sins, and, most importantly, an almighty God that was all that is good. A book was often referenced as proof of all this, but no one really knew how its chapters came to be written. They said it came from God. I had studied other religions, and many followed this general pattern. I was taught that non-believers would lie, cheat, steal, and kill for their own benefit if they could get away with it, having no god to answer to. Now here I was sitting in the Crystal Palace Restaurant, talking with this non-believer, and he did not fit the mold I had been told was cast for him. He was a virtuous man, he loved people and helped them if he could, he was honest, and he had never killed anyone, as many believers were doing in that time of war.

Why did he live this way? Wasn't it more satisfying and pleasurable to just grab what you want? His answer, of course, was no. He did not get satisfaction from greed, or security from killing, or confidence in criticizing, or joy in jealousy, or self-worth from power. He was a good person because it made him happy and that was its own reward. This made great sense to me, but was it possible? What rules did you follow? How did you always know the right thing to do? How could you be sure that you wouldn't hurt someone? So many doubts when there was no structure to follow.

Our conversation ended, and I left feeling a little weird. Goodness without God was weird. I was a believer and I tried to be reasonably good because of what I was taught. Here was a non-believer who could be any way he pleased, yet he also strove to be good.

Forty years later there is little left of what I was taught. I no longer believe in God because of what is written in a book or what I am told. I have come to live more like my non-believer friend. If someone now asked me if I believe in God, I could not accurately say yes, not because I don't believe in God, but because for me this concept of belief in the universally accepted idea of God just doesn't fit. What does fit is the universal power of love which my friend discovered before he knew it was God.

Number Three

Faith

When I was young, I did not think of faith at all. I was taught stuff and that was it. Later it was just a matter of figuring out which stuff was fantasy and which was real. Faith was not a factor, and I never understood exactly what it is. Unlike using the brain to logically think something through to an important conclusion (which, although at times quite difficult, is possible) thinking oneself to faith is impossible.
Or is it?

We assume our brains generate all of our thoughts and subsequent actions and the rest is supported by the universe. A friend Steve espoused predestination. He argued that everything was generated by what came before it, right down to what you decide to have for breakfast today or who rules the world. I understood his argument, but in practice it seemed to me impossible for anyone to live by this theory. For all practical purposes, people go about life making decisions. So, how does one make a decision to believe in something beyond the temporal? If I were still arguing with Steve, I would ask what in the physical universe of predestination could cause you to arrive at something like faith that is beyond the physical? I was convinced of existence beyond the temporal when I went to the limit of my mind and saw the impossibility of there not being more. So I have little use for either Steve's limiting theory of predestination or the more common illogical leap of faith. For me, faith is not believing in something I cannot know, but rather trusting that what I do not understand, understands me.   Life is. Existence is. My job is to figure out how to live and at the same time allow myself to exist.

Part Two

Opinion

Number One

The Bible

Any sensible person who reads the Bible or other ancient book, the purpose of which is to reveal or teach things spiritual, should be troubled if they truly seek the spirit. The limits of the mind of the writers or translators and the agendas of perhaps less than innocent manipulators, sometimes makes the choice of words somewhat removed from the truths they seek to reveal. My advice is to let these words fall on your ears as all words should do, to be valued by each person and allow spiritual truth come from the soul of your being.

Number Two

God

Before I muse about God, I feel compelled to improve my vocabulary in respect to the name God. The fact that I prefer cats to dogs as a pet does not mean that I don't have the greatest respect for dogs. Cats just seem to be more efficient, and my wife finds them cuddly and comforting. I think that when referring to an entity that is supposed to be everything, there could be a better name. For the present purpose I will use the word One.[1] It sounds like what it's supposed to be and some preconceptions may be avoided.

It makes no sense to believe in One. To say that there must be some power that began our universe, and the possible universes beyond ours, does make some sense since something cannot sensibly come from nothing. If you call that power One, then it does make sense to believe in One. However, to believe in an interacting one, as most people do, does not make sense. Living beings, lacking any metaphysical communication, have no sensible reason to believe that One interacts with them. If someone believes this they must have some other reason, using some other capacity.

The element of our being that would impart this non-scientific theoretical capacity may be your spirit. If we are not only flesh but also spirit, and if there is an interacting

---

[1] The whole is the sum of its parts. If you believe God is everything, and you could add up the fractional values of all things, the sum would be one.

One, then any realization of One would lie in the spirit part and would not be accessible by the senses.

There may have been a quasi-sensible reason for a mind to believe, and that is if someone was lucky enough to have personally met Jesus or another person who claimed to be a direct physical manifestation of One, who, upon request, delivered a bona fide metaphysical event. In that case, the mind could reasonably believe that One is personal. Lacking this direct metaphysical experience, we must rely on hearsay of such events, which necessitates believing the hearsayer. That is not an option and we are left with no verifiable sensory evidence.

But what if your normal physical experiences are not just experiences but have metaphysical purpose? And what if the spirit knows this purpose even if the mind does not? And what if the spirit has the power to communicate with both the mind and the elusive One…?

If personal experience, no matter what its frame of reference, causes your mind to overload enough times (once may be enough for some people), you begin to doubt not your temporal experience but the limits. At that point, whether something makes sense or not, does not matter. What matters is that there is "something" that's more exciting than sensory experience, and it may have something to do with One. I for one want to "experience" as much of it as possible.

Number Three

Jesus

When I was a young man in college, I took a course in comparative religion, but I really don't remember much about religions. Having been raised a Catholic, I do know a little about that particular religion. This lack of knowledge, however, is not that limiting with regard to any Christian religion since its only important factor would be the central character. Given that believing in a divine Jesus can not be a sensible process, unless one has physically met him, then the only sensible approach is to examine the independently verified facts. To my knowledge there are only a few.

⇒ There definitely was an historical man named more or less Jesus.
⇒ He was executed by the Romans for ostensibly causing trouble within his Jewish religion.
⇒ He impressed a relatively large number of people.

My opinion is that he must have caused a major stir to be admired by many and yet be killed off by the establishment. He probably did claim to be a direct messenger of God or King of the Jews or equal with the Father or the like, and that is why he got bumped off. But others throughout history have made similar fantastic claims, and they have been ignored as lunatics. Jesus must have had a pretty good act to have made such an impact, and he must have known it. Therefore, in my opinion he was either:

⇒ one of history's best con artists;
⇒ an extremely persuasive delusional lunatic; or
⇒ exactly what he claimed to be.

Part Three

Experiences

Number One

The First Time

When I was a young boy, I tried to be good. Having been raised a Catholic, "good" meant following the rules and rituals, which I attempted to do to the letter.

After exactly midnight every Saturday night, no food entered my mouth until after mass the next day. It made sense to me in the remote event that something you ate would disagree with you while at church and you puked up God after receiving Holy Communion.

The best reason for fasting was not Sunday mass but "First Friday." On the first Friday of each month, there was a special mass before school in the morning with the required midnight fast. This mass seemed to have longer periods of kneeling than Sunday mass, but this was probably not the case. It only seemed that way because what came after mass was what made "First Friday" worth it, even though the blood sometimes drained out of your brain and you began to sweat just before you lost consciousness from low blood sugar. After mass, there was a table piled with box after box of Krispy Kreme doughnuts and crates of individual cartons of chocolate milk. For a ten-year-old, there was no better high than all that sugar and a little caffeine on an empty stomach right after swallowing God.

Not all the rules and rituals were this much fun. Some were totally practical; others were relics of the past with little or no current meaning; others seemed to be dreamed up by some sexual pervert; some may even have helped one attain love. No matter whether they were ridiculous or sublime, I was a good boy and I religiously followed them all. I didn't have to think. I didn't have to worry what the right thing to do was. I didn't even have to make up my own prayers. For that rule-following ten-year-old boy, life was easy.

I followed the rules and rituals for several years. One summer after I had become an altar boy, I was asked to do some private altar boy work at a priest's home. This priest impressed me because I had no idea that some priests' jobs were to travel around doing important good works rather than the usual parish work. This priest lived in his own house, complete with stereo, 27 inch television, library – the works. He also had the title of Monsignor. His priestly garb was not black, but a kind of purplish magenta. Whenever I saw him, however, he always wore slacks and a T-shirt. All of this was definitely very cool and in part influenced me to consider becoming a priest. I thought it would be a good thing to do.

And so, I went to the seminary after grade school. It was a minor seminary. There was no real priestly stuff yet, just school work and sports. God had something to do with it, but that was just part of the rules and rituals. Stories were told of how this person or that saint had heard the word of God, but with all my goodness and rule-following, something inside of me would say, "Yeah, sure!" Although I recited many prayers that were supposed to be communication with God, they were a one-sided communication. If God was listening, I wasn't expecting any answers. I didn't need any. The rules and rituals said it all, and that was fine with me.

When I returned to the seminary after a summer break to begin my third year, it happened for the first time. It was on the third or fourth night back during the grand silence, which began after evening prayers in the chapel and ended after morning prayers again in the chapel. As you walked to the dormitory, brushed your teeth, put on your pajamas, etc., you remained completely silent. This of course was not always the case. Sometimes after "lights out" and the prefect had gone to bed, all hell would break loose, but that's another story. This night, all was quiet. I had retired to my bed and was fast falling asleep when I chanced to think one more informal prayer, and it happened. It wasn't a conversation, but if it were, it would have gone something like this:

God: "Hello!"
Me: "Hello?!"
God: "Why are you here?"
Me: "Isn't this what I'm supposed to be doing?"
God: "Not really."
Me: "Okay…"

The next day, when I informed the headmaster of my sudden decision to leave the seminary, he asked me if I was sure. Oh yes, I was quite sure. I made no mention that last night was my first time. On that night the slow dismantling of my rules and rituals began.

Number Two

Altered Mind

As a very young man (just beginning to figure out my own beliefs and how they relate to my life) it was important to examine all the possibilities with as little prejudice as possible. My ultimate truths no longer came packaged by others to be read and believed. Although many traditional values seemed reasonably good, others were obviously flawed. Truths now had to come from within.

Experience is a great tool in discovering truth, perhaps the only one for a human. Some of the more painful experiences are best acquired secondhand, if one has that choice. The less painful and the more pleasant ones, on the other hand, can be evaluated personally, although not always without some danger or discomfort along with the benefits.

Sex, drugs, rock and roll, speed, power, love, generosity, fame, wealth, success, failure, sickness, health; pain, knowledge, sports, nature, dreams, habits, culture, food, science, politics, art, friends and foes-- the list of possible experiences that could lead to some understanding of life and its purpose is as long as one's imagination will allow.

One potentially dangerous category is drugs, specifically mind-altering ones. Drugs in general are used by nearly everyone, and mind-altering ones, both prescription and non, are used in varying degrees by many.

My first experience with altered reality was probably spinning around as a child until I was so dizzy I couldn't stand up. This is not exactly a pleasant experience, but the rush was such that it did require some investigation. It is soon evident, even to a child, that experiences like this one are of little value. Longer lasting mind-alterations that interact not only with the senses but also the emotions and are deemed in some way pleasurable or beneficial require considerably more investigation.

The altered state various drugs produce we generally refer to as a high, and at first blush they do seem to raise certain levels of awareness if administered in the correct dosage. After several years of occasional research in my late teens and early twenties, I came to a relatively sudden conclusion. It occurred to me that, although the colors seemed brighter, the music seemed clearer, the snacks seemed tastier, the friends seemed friendlier, art was more inspiring, nature seemed more natural, and jokes seemed funnier, something less temporal faded in the process. Something I had been barely aware of in my daily routine became a downer in its absence. Several follow-up experiments yielded the same results. I was definitely higher when I was not high, so I ceased all chemical research.

Over the years, this previously under-appreciated higher state has persisted through better and worse. At times, I have shoved it largely into my subconscious, and at other times I have tried to allow it to elevate my state of being. It can best be described, though not explained, as awareness of spirit. Not long ago, this higher state increased in intensity spontaneously and it definitely requires considerable investigation.

Number Three

The Air Conditioner

In my twenties, I began a health food restaurant. I purchased an existing business, and my first wife was to be the cook. We used nearly all of our start-up money for the down payment, and with the help of many volunteer friends, we transformed a failing greasy spoon into a funky hangout in seven days and opened for business with no money in the bank. The previous owner had guaranteed in the purchase agreement that all the equipment, though very old, was in working condition. This was technically true, but it was very fortunate that I loved to fix things.

We opened the restaurant in February of 1973, and it took off right away, meaning that we were serving about 100 people a day and grossing over $200, which was at least $50 more per day than I had calculated we would need to break even. The rent was $450 per month.

Four months later when summer arrived, I attempted to turn on the old Westinghouse air conditioner after some instruction from Bob, my irreverent and wise-cracking repairman. When I threw the handle of the knife switch on the wall above the unit, it came to life like a jackhammer and scared the hell out of me. It worked, but barely.

The compressor was a six cylinder water cooler unit that was powered by a 20 horsepower internal motor. It stood 4 feet high and 6 feet long and looked like a large diesel engine. It was located in the basement of the building and was installed when the building was constructed in 1932. The noise now emanating from it was so loud it could be heard upstairs in the dining room right through the eight inch concrete floor. After 2 weeks, as the temperature outside edged towards ninety degrees, the unit shut itself off. "Bob, help!" I screamed in the phone. When he arrived, he hit the reset button after a short inspection and shook his head as the unit roared back to life. It ran for a short time and then shut itself off again. It was totally worn out from 40 years of use. Repair was out of the question, far too much labor to be cost effective and a new unit installed on the roof would cost $10,000, also out of the question. Bob was sympathetic to my plight but there was nothing that could be done – except…. He smiled his irreverent smile, "I'm not officially telling you this, but if you bypass the overload safety cut-off, you may be able to make it run a little longer." There was no other choice, and so I tried it. If I could only make it last the summer, maybe by next year I would have enough money to replace it.

Every day I cringed as it roared to life ever louder and louder until after two weeks or so the three main 100 amp. fuses blew. Inside the six cylinder sealed compressor, the bearings had chewed themselves to pieces and the huge internal motor had literally burned up, even in its cooling bath of Freon, and had locked solid. We were faced with financial disaster.

I thought back to when I was 15 years old. The transmission on my *Lambretta 150* motor scooter had broken. I could not afford to have it repaired, so with the help of a shop manual I attempted to fix it myself. As I gazed at the internal workings of the transmission, I marveled at its design. I could never have invented something like that, but I realized that I sure as hell could fix it, and I did. Now, faced with this disaster, I called the Westinghouse factory to see if I could obtain a repair manual. I was going to fix it myself.

After a short time, a copy of the 40 year-old manual was located. I called my brother, a physicist, to enlist his help, and also my brother-in-law, and anyone else who was willing to get their hands dirty. The story of that repair would take many chapters to detail, but the repair itself, though time-consuming, was not really that complicated. Take it apart, rewind the motor, replace all the bearings, and reassemble. The problem was that since I had bypassed the safety, when the motor burned up, its rotor (which weighed about 75 pounds) had "welded" itself onto its tapered shaft and refused to be removed. Every attempt to remove it failed. I tried every trick I knew and every suggestion offered to no avail. I connected steel rods to the rotor and attached them to a screw type impact puller that was tightened with a sledge hammer by pounding on the puller's steel lever arm. The steel rods soon snapped but the rotor would not budge. I replaced the broken rods with new ones made of stronger chromium steel, and we pounded on that puller for weeks. We sprayed the rotor with WD-40 and let it soak for days at a time. We heated it with a blow torch while we pounded. Someone I barely knew with huge muscles and confidence to match took a turn with the sledge hammer but left exhausted and defeated. One by one, everyone gave up.

It was nearly August and Washington summer was at its height. The temperatures were in the nineties nearly every day and with DC's typical humidity, it drove people indoors to air-conditioned comfort. The indoor temperature of my restaurant however rose at times to 110 degrees. The customers all went elsewhere. A few loyal souls straggled back in if a rain shower cooled things down a bit, but it seemed hopeless. Two more months of heat and we would be out of business.

I went down into the basement one last time alone. All the helpers were gone. There was nothing more to try. I climbed behind the compressor as I had done hundreds of times before and sat down on the milk crate facing the stubborn rotor. I picked up the sledgehammer and pounded with all my might, slamming the eight pound steel head of the hammer again and again against the arm of the puller until my muscles ached with exhaustion. Then I stopped. It was over. I had tried everything and had failed, and now the restaurant would have to close. This was sad; the restaurant seemed like such a good thing.

I sat for some time on that milk crate dripping with sweat and thinking. There was something here for me to see, but I had been trying so hard I had not stopped to look until now.

I had always been a spiritually-centered person. I believed that one should live their life to the best of their abilities and then hopefully move on to the pure spirit level. I believed that spirit did have some relationship with the temporal, but a direct attempt to apply the spirit to the physical had not been part of my behavior since the formula prayers of my youth. Now here was the physical stretched to its limit; why not try going beyond it? It's hard to explain exactly how I did this, but the prayer had no words. Whatever it was, I would allow it to happen. I had no belief that anything physical would actually occur.

Staring at the rotor I felt something inside me. I slowly picked up the sledge hammer from the concrete floor and gently tapped the puller arm one last time. My body lurched and I dropped the hammer as the 75 pound rotor came sliding towards me. My heart beating so fast, I could hardly hold the rotor from falling onto the concrete.

When I had regained some small amount of composure, I shoved a broom handle through the center of the rotor and carried it triumphantly upstairs. My tears were not of joy but of amazement. "How?" the question was asked, and I could only mumble, "I don't know how! It just happened when I…."

Over 26 years later, when my restaurant had run its course and it was time to sell the business to a new owner, the rent was nearly $9,000 per month and that air conditioner was still running. I did not tell the new owners the story of the air conditioner. I just told them that they would have to replace it because it was running on a wing and a prayer.

Number Four

The Accident

In my senior year at Fordham College in Bronx, New York, I worked a part-time job at Reliable Hardware Store on White Plains Road, several miles from my apartment. I was riding my motorcycle, a 1960 *Yamaha YDS1*, home from work one evening. I stopped in the left lane at a red light on a side street under the elevated subway tracks that run north/south above Webster Ave. I intended to make a left turn to the south as I did each night and then ride the final mile or so home. When the light changed to green, I did not start out right away. After seven or eight years of riding, I had already developed a fairly good defensive attitude, and I knew better than to cross three lanes of traffic until I was sure they had plenty of time to stop. I waited several seconds and then proceeded into the intersection with my left hand signaling the turn. Suddenly from between the stopped traffic on my left there roared a large white car, its driver making a drunken attempt to beat the light long since turned red. He must have slammed on his brakes before he hit me because a 30 mph broadside would have crippled me. As it was, his bumper slammed into my left leg which smashed into my gas tank and sent both me and the bike splattering to the pavement. I lay there for several minutes on my back looking up at the elevated tracks above, rain drizzling on my face, my helmet cradling my head. It was peaceful in a way. I felt no pain. When I did move, my leg was numb. I got up slowly and stumbled to a nearby bar to call my wife. The leg felt huge and unreal with each limping step as some sensation returned. When the ambulance arrived, I began to feel very lucky. It could have been so much worse. In fact, X-rays later showed that somehow my bones remained intact.

Twenty-five years later, I was riding my 1982 *Suzuki GS650G* home from my restaurant one evening. There was a light rain falling. I was traveling north on Massachusetts Avenue, which has two lanes of traffic in each direction. My face shield was spotted with raindrops that distorted the light from the headlights as they approached. Stopped in the left lane at an uncontrolled intersection with my turn signal on to make a left turn, I was facing uphill. The approaching traffic was traveling downhill at well over the posted 30 mph speed limit. I watched each car's headlights approach and pass by until the road turned black and empty. Slowly beginning my turn, looking toward the side street onto which I was heading, I glanced casually to my right up Massachusetts Avenue expecting to see two long empty lanes all the way to the next intersection at Wisconsin Avenue 200 yards away. It is amazing how much processing a brain can do in a fraction of a second. I can still see the unlit headlights, the grill, the bumper, even the license plate. I can still remember my brain subconsciously calculating the car's velocity and the 15 or 20 feet distance between it and me. I can still feel my body defensively tense itself for the inevitable. This was going to be bad, very bad. My brain gave a final desperate order to my right wrist to twist the throttle on full. I can still hear the surprisingly small metallic sound of the hit; it felt like the car went right through me. My next memory was braking to a stop at the curb on the side street, dazed and confused.

A Good Samaritan pulled up next to me and rolled down his window. "Are you okay??" he asked, also seeming confused to see me still upright. He had been traveling from behind me and had made a U-turn a little way up Massachusetts Avenue to come back and help. I assured him that I was okay. "But I saw you get hit," he said, seeking some explanation. I had none. The car had hit me on my right muffler; the dent is still visible. After my first accident, I felt lucky. This time I felt something more than luck.

Number Five

The Dream

I have not studied dreams and I do not spend a lot of time trying to interpret my dreams; I just enjoy them. I have never to my knowledge had a nightmare. When a nightmare type dream begins, a feeling of power takes over and counteracts the fear necessary for a nightmare. In one dream I had, a woman who I did not know, is alone in an empty pit in a state of total despair. The woman becomes aware of my presence and desperately lunges toward me, becoming 10 or 15 feet tall. It is not so much she who is trying to engulf me, but the despair itself. It is impossible to describe the intensity of this despair, but if it were unleashed in real life, even a sane person might kill himself to escape it. As the despair envelops me and seems to suck at my soul, I have a feeling of confidence and love that I attempt to impart to the woman. The despair retreats with the woman to the far end of the pit and she cowers in agony, the despair eating at her but finding no satisfaction. I awake feeling sad for that poor soul. There have been only a few dreams like this; most of my dreams are fun. In my youth, they were largely unintelligible fantasy, but as I grow older, they are almost always recognizable if not always comprehensible. There are a few recurrent unrealistic elements, like the ability to fly or willfully break any physical law you so wish. But now mostly my dreams are a somewhat sensible processing of some day's events.

One dream, however, and only one, was something very different. I will probably spend the rest of my life wondering where it came from and trying not so much to understand it as to live it.

It was a quick and simple dream. I was walking near a number of other people who I did not know. One person walking with these people came to my attention. He was dressed in a one piece off-white tunic and he spoke to me, saying these exact words in the following order: "I am God. You have power you never even dreamed of. You will develop a devotion to the Eucharist."

I woke up immediately and mentally exclaimed in the direction of the dream, Ho-leee shit! God? No way! Power? What power? He ended a sentence with a preposition for crissake. What in god's name did he mean by the Eucharist?

Number Six

The Game

I'm sure I am not the only one who has played this game. It's quite simple to play on the surface. Begin with your individual surroundings; imagine that they don't exist and expand that thought in whatever increments appeal to you, until the possibility that all of temporal existence does not exist. This can be done in one step by imagining before the big bang, but that's not as effective. When you have reached this non-temporal state, what remains is the incomprehensibility of God if you are a believer or the endless possibility of the unknown if you are not. The last step is to remove either God or the unknown. Game over! It's much more fun for believers. Removing the unknown just doesn't have the same kick as removing God.

Although these steps are simple, the hard part is to actually experience each feeling. When you remove something from existence, you must experience only what is left. If you take the long route by eliminating smaller things first and progressing to larger, at some point you will eliminate the planet Earth. You would still be left with quite a bit, virtually 100% of the universe, but to an earthling this is a big step. If you are playing the game correctly, you should get at least a slight buzz. When you get to the elimination of the entire universe, it should feel scary with nothing familiar to hang on to. The final elimination would bring you to nothing that is impossible for the mind to comprehend. The experience of attempting this is awesome. When the mind blows, the overload seems to stretch to infinity, and the rush is heart-stopping.

When I was young, I could play the game at will, although a period of recovery was necessary after each game. The effect of the game on me, aside from the awesome rush, was the secure conviction that although it was possible to mentally eliminate an awful lot, maybe even your own self, it was impossible to eliminate existence itself.

I stopped playing the game when I was no longer young. Much later in life I remember trying the game again. I was about 45 years old. It still sort of worked, but the intensity was disappointing -- no big climax, just a little shiver. Fast forward to the present. I just tried the game again. Nothing. Nothing at all! I don't mean I reached the elusive nothing, but that I could no longer play the game. I dutifully went through the steps but nothing happened. In a way this is just as exciting. What is different? I realize now that it is doubt. You need some doubt to play the game, and evidently too much of my doubt has been destroyed by the many experiences of my life and maybe even the game itself.

Without having doubt, the game becomes one of addition instead of subtraction. The steps now are to realize that the tiny individual is part of an ever-increasing reality until it becomes aware of and part of the God or the unknown reality.

Part Four

Other BS

Although these words are peppered with humor, the occasional obscenity, and probably a little heresy, they are no more or no less useless to the discerning eye than all the pious and flowery words, not that there is anything wrong with pious and flowery words if you like that sort of thing.

For many, religion is security. Sometimes in that security one loses sight of the truth. Religion, no matter how important, is still only a tool. All security and truth must come from within.

I was taught that if you did not observe something personally, no matter how lofty the secondary source, it is merely hearsay or opinion. Whether there is any truth in it is up to each individual to divine.

Believing in God is not sensible. It is not arrived at by direct use of the senses. However, there are sensible reasons why you would want to engage in such behavior if you define God, as love.
    Expressing this love to someone, whether a friend or a stranger, feels good for whatever reason.

There are no harmful side effects, unless you try to apply it to someone forcibly, in which case it's not really love but more like hate.

It's free.

It's more fun than the alternative that doesn't make any sense either.

Unlike the alternative, there is no way to lose.

Spiritual love lies beneath the surface emotions. When you emotionally love, it is easy to imagine that this spiritual love emanates from your soul and could conquer petty emotions. But try it a few times when there is a temptation to hate. It's worth trying.

To deal with your emotions from highs that seek joy and ecstasy to lows that threaten hate and death, find a key to the spirit and use it every minute you can.

I don't pray. When requested, I will mouth the words while mostly trying to get beyond their distraction. I do find it meditative to attempt to understand the words of the "Our Father," but that's not praying. When I was young, what I considered my spiritual life consisted almost entirely of prayer. There were prayers for every occasion. Prayers of asking were primary, and if they worked, prayers of thanks were in order. Prayers of contrition were kind of forced on you lest you burn in Purgatory or, worse, Hell. Prayers of praise were a bit confusing; like it was necessary for you to make God feel good as opposed to Him feeling bad or getting pissed off if you didn't? Prayers of awe were probably the most accurate for me if I had thought about it.

There were some rather creative prayers of self-deprecation that I suspect were more about the person than about prayer. Some prayers, especially ones in the Bible, were scary as hell, about killing and hate and an avenging God. It was enough to make anyone swear off praying completely. But that is not why I don't pray.

Gary Null, a natural health advocate, among many other things, conducted an experiment on prayers. If I remember correctly, he asked respected elders from four different religions to pray over some bean sprouts to see what the result would be. In all four cases the sprouts that were prayed over grew considerably faster than a control portion of sprouts. If you have heard of Gary you would know that he is meticulous in his attention to accuracy, so this result was no fluke. Apparently something in the attitude of those praying had a positive effect. Plants don't lie. But I still don't pray. If I did, I would only be thinking in the back of my mind about the poor sprouts that God ignored because I was praying for the competition.

The key for me is not prayer but that attitude, that state of spirit. Words are optional, useful perhaps if one wishes to hear oneself pray. My key can be expressed in two words – allow love.

Part Five

Love Poems

Introduction

For many, it is reassuring to picture God as our Father in Heaven or some other all-powerful benevolent being that exists in some unseen place. But God is most surely the love that can exist in every soul, and if one allows that love to exist, it has the power to quietly amaze.

I don't like love poems. I like motorcycles and such. The first of these poems however, I do like. I made it up over 40 years ago. The rest of them I was forced to write just yesterday.

FOR JOY

FOR JOY FOR JOY FOR SHIT

I SEE NO USE IN IT

SUCH THINGS I SEE MUST BE

AND LITTLE PUPS MUST PEE

   I GUESS

FOR JOY FOR JOY THE HELL

WHAT IS THAT RANCID SMELL

IT IS THE BASTARD LIFE

WITH ALL HIS FUCKIN STRIFE

FOR JOY FOR JOY FOR LOVE

FOR LOVE FOR LOVE FOR LOVE

ECSTATIC LOVE

One night I dreamt of love
That melted down my life
Surrender beyond all thought
And when I awoke
It still burned within
Did I love or was I loved

INDEPENDENT LOVE

Love needs no frame of pretty words
Love needs no understanding
Love cares not if you are afraid
Love cares not how we're breathing
For love can live as we define
Or love can live transforming
With love we search that fearful place
From love this life gains meaning

SELFISH LOVE

The mountain that is moved by love
Is not the mountain that I see
And selfish though it is to want
I still ask love for it to be

CAN'T BUY ME LOVE

Can't buy me love
And stash it away
To get satisfaction
To enjoy every day
Love is for giving
That's what we say
So that's what I do
And it does seem to pay

QUIET LIGHT

Last night I saw that light again
Quiet like the very early dawn
Persistent though
Like the songbird's chirp
Pleasing my soul
Sometimes I wish the night would never end
For in the light of day
That quiet light
Persistent though
Too often I ignore

SEARCHING FOR LOVE

We search the book and word and rule
And thus become confused
Afraid to think and question why
We simply force to choose
As if the truth were written down
With perfect wit and rhyme
With knowledge of the only truth
Explained for just one time
It's not the book or word or rule
Where answers you will find
It's in the love of your own heart
And not some hallowed mind
So when in book and word and rule
The answers you demand
Look also in your own pure heart
That peace is in your hand
It's not so hard to set life free
Just love and let love be

BECOMING LOVE

If life were a garden of Eden
With never a sorrow or pain
And success were automatic
With nothing ever to gain
If love were given for us
And life were not a game
The joy it would be endless
But would it be the same
It would be someone else's life
And not our life to live
And we would not become the self
That feels the love to give
It seems we must have love to lose
To be the one to choose

LOVE POWER

When life is cozy and abundant
It's easy to allow love
When life is terrible and destroyed
How great the one who loves
Would I ever want that test
I don't think so … yet
Imagine the power
Of love with no worldly reason
Is my fear so strong
That I would shy away
Were I to be forsaken
Such time would never come for me
But if it ever did
I wonder what would be
The mettle of my love

ONLY LOVE

If life has no rhyme or reason
That I can understand
Then why so well defined
We demand certainty, yet
With all the knowledge
Man has acquired
We still are certain
Of almost nothing
Yet we kill to possess
A crumb of reality
Which will fade to nothing
Give that crumb to your neighbor
Or a stranger
And this reality
Becomes a great power
Why is it so hard to do
And it surely is
The illusion is that if
We beat the competition
We will become king
King of what
We don't even understand
With power to destroy
Only yourself
I guess fear is the driver
And we think
With possessions or power
The fear will cease
Has it ever

Part Six

More BS

I have been blessed with a full stomach and a clear mind. For this reason, I cannot follow blindly nor run wantonly, but sit and listen to reality and tell what I hear.

My spiritual belief is simple: the source of existence (aka, God) is love and by allowing love you become a unique and unending part of reality.

Allowing love is the answer? Is it that simple? Still, my logical mind wonders, why is there pain and suffering? My upbringing was Christian, and even the Christ who by Christian belief is this love, had pain and suffering. I have experienced some small amount and it does not seem to have had any effect on my capacity to accept love. If an evil person is the cause of the pain, it becomes a little more difficult. There can be a desire to "kill" that person especially if the pain is directed at a loved one. As difficult as it seems to accept in those circumstances, I am convinced that accepting love is the only satisfactory answer. With any other answer, I would still feel miserable. With this accepting, although my emotion feels pain, love remains illogically untouched. It has yet to fail. I have a screaming desire to know why but, somehow I understand the answer is always to allow love.

We are not the source of love. We are the fountain.

Just because someone's words are syrupy and filled with unrealistic optimism, does not necessarily mean that they are the ranting of a fairy tale. Likewise, do not fear irreverence that may shake your security. By accepting love in any form we make our reality.

Everything becomes boring when repeated over and over unless there is no boredom to begin with, in which case it becomes more desirable with each repetition.

I don't believe in anything, neither do I disbelieve. I know only what I experience and my understanding of that is superficial at best. But my salvation is that I experience love, and it grabs me hard. If I allow, it destroys my fear, satisfies my greed, fulfills my passion, softens my anger, feeds my compassion, laughs at my vanity, cooks my dinner and takes out my trash in more ways than one.

If one believes, they always seek to reassure. If one knew, imagine the power.

Change what you can, love what you can't.

If you're blamin' the devil for doin' his job, then you ain't doin' yours.

When I am presented with a problem primarily of the mathematical type, I may or may not have the intelligence to figure it out, but I definitely lack the discipline. Instead, I will just plug in answers until one works, and then maybe come up with some vague idea of why. It seems that I have done the same with my life, and now that I have found the universal answer of allowing love, I go about like some smart ass who has the correct answer to every problem.

However, until I have a good idea why, perhaps I shall continue seeking like Prairie Home Companion's Guy Noir until senility completely overtakes me.

Life's persistent questions:
How? Interesting to think about, but it really doesn't matter
Where? Mostly here, but also there and everywhere
Why? Why not
Who? You and me
When? Now
What? Love

I think that life is ruled by logic that can randomly give joy or cause pain. Man is in a constant attempt to tip the balance in his favor. However, this logic has little effect on whether a person is a giver or a taker. Something beyond logic does have this power.

Everyone wants to be heard. Everyone has something to say. Some are afraid to speak. Others never shut up. The hardest thing to do is listen to more than the words, especially your own.

Upon considering not provable ideas
Why are we sometimes upset by the spiritual ideas of others, when ultimately only the truth exists? A lie is not an idea and an incorrect idea does not affect the truth. Are we afraid that belief in some idea may cause someone to act harmfully? This is a legitimate fear and explains why we make laws to control actions. However, an idea when left in the idea state, can cause no harm. Discomfort should only

happen if we believe a disturbing idea. And why would we do that? If someone else's belief in a correct idea causes us discomfort, then the cause of the discomfort lies with us, not the idea. If someone's belief in what we would consider a fantasy causes us discomfort, then we must not be secure in our own belief.

Sometimes when I read the news I hope to see a miracle, but I know we are the miracle.

Sarcastic people like me who make fun of the idea of an invisible Man in the sky should not always be dismissed as irreverent non-believers. I believe there is what most people call God just like I know there is something remotely like infinitesimal vibrating strings that are making life seem real. The fact that billions and billions of particles are zooming straight through the earth and not bumping into anything because the earth, like most all matter, is made up of mostly empty space, doesn't make me feel like the earth doesn't really exist. Likewise, the fact that I can't pick up a pitcher of love and pour a glass doesn't make me feel like love doesn't exist. So I make fun of the common beliefs that the temporal state is real and that God is an invisible Man in the sky because what will remain when all ideas have played out their illusion, is love.

The universe is astronomically large and infinitesimally small. Beyond these parameters lies love and by our will It lies within as well.

The capacity of existence is not measured by the circumstances of life, whether perceived to be good or bad, but by the will to love regardless.

Life is an illusion but it's a real illusion.

When I try to comprehend reality, it feels like I'm trying to do higher mathematics on a pocket calculator. I am amazed by the ultimate reality. Abandoned by understanding, a feeling quietly overloads my brain and all it can do is silently repeat to whoever is listening, "Ho-lee shit!"

Our lives play out like stories in a book and become history, or were they history before they began, determined by our capacity to love and existing forever?

Quantum love
Science can accept the word spirit to describe the pre-existing state before the theoretical big bang, and even wonders if there is some observable effect of this "force" on the temporal that might help formulate quantum theory. But science stops far short of suggesting that any intellect could communicate with this force. It is left to the religions and spiritual seekers of the world to attempt this communication. There are a wide variety of practices, some contradictory, that we claim are successful at this communication. To my mind, this is not a problem, since quantum theory "believes" that certain particles can be in two places at once.

The important thing in our attempts is to be careful not to invent the object of our attempts. Since this force lies outside understanding, science looks for the effect by this force on a particle, and we look for an effect of this force in communication. For me, this force is reality that must be approached without definition. Call it what works for you, but putting a limit on it is like trying to locate a particle in quantum space. I call it love, and I try not to define it or be frustrated in an attempt to locate its position. Rather, I try to let it be everywhere. Someday, I may attempt to articulate a quantum theory of love but it surely wouldn't be very scientific, although maybe if I were a whole lot smarter it could be.

Slowly we advance our knowledge and primitive mastery of the physical while scientific law remains a comforting, though mind-boggling, constant. The spiritual is advanced by the simple act of giving love. It is its only law and our only real power.

I guess there's no harm in inventing words and ideas to express your God. Will those ideas hold true when your God has forsaken you (Matt 27-46)? Will you condemn your fellow man when his words of God challenge yours? When you accept love, there are no definitions and your ideas become as dreams in their attempt to define the experience. My advice is to listen to your words of love that have not been written, for the written words give comfort to your ear, but when you are forsaken only the word of love speaks to every soul.

The dream revisited
When I had that one dream some 20 years ago I didn't understanding 2 out of the 3 statements. The first statement being an introduction required no understanding; not that I understand what God is but there are plenty of definitions to choose from. If I hadn't yet chosen love when I had the dream, I certainly have now.

The second statement, rather than requiring understanding, needs only acceptance. I choose to believe that the power referred to is the power of love. If someday I acquire a fuller understanding of it, all the better.

The third statement was the real problem for me. The Webster's New World Dictionary was the best dictionary I had and it's only definition of Eucharist was "consecrated bread and wine used in Holy Communion." I just couldn't see myself devoted to a superficial piece of bread or slug of wine even if it does become God and is a fantastically effective gimmick. Although I did make a few periodic futile attempts at devotion as I became increasingly aware of love, the only devotion to bread I could see myself developing was a taste for toasted spelt bread sprayed with butter flavor and sprinkled with crushed flax seeds, and the only wine I simply must have is a glass of red whenever I eat pasta. Therefore, I looked instead to a phrase that I had often heard, "the Eucharistic body of Christ." I definitely could see myself devoted to the love of every being in this Eucharistic body, although the enormity of that entity is quite intimidating. So I have approached it one being at a time with some success, but I couldn't really say I have developed a devotion to it, rather I just do it.

The thing that I seemed to be more and more focused on was my relationship to love. It was not only something I tried to do because it was pleasurable to me, and hopefully to those I loved, but rather something that just was. It sat there deep inside like a beating heart. I don't know if you can say one becomes devoted to his heart for keeping him alive, but I surely had developed a pretty strong attachment to the presence of love.

Several days ago, my spelling ability failed me as it often does, and I grabbed the old copy of Webster's Collegiate Dictionary that I keep near the computer for just that purpose. If I need a good definition I use the big, more inclusive, New World edition. I plopped the book open to look for a certain word, and I happened to see the word Eucharist. I casually looked at the familiar definition of bread and wine etc. and then I saw something the big dictionary lacked - definition #2. It was the Christian Science definition and it read *"SPIRITUAL COMMUNION WITH THE ONE GOD."* Bingo!

I don't pray, but if I did, it would probably sound something like this:

Source of existence I (or we) humbly address you
May your love be shared in the world as it is in reality
Give me what I need today and pardon my offenses
As I will pardon those who offend me
And so that I may not be tempted by a life of illusion
Or consumed by evil
Lead me to love

Brother Bob

(contactbrotherbob@verizon.net)
***

Trust that what you don't understand, understands you

Giving love is our only real power

The job is to find out how to live and allow yourself to exist

<u>Allow love</u>

www.ingramcontent.com/pod-product-compliance
Lightning Source LLC
Chambersburg PA
CBHW051713040426
42446CB00008B/865